MW01377686

BRAZIL

Written by Doug Barone

PowerKiDS press™

Published in 2025
by The Rosen Publishing Group, Inc.
2544 Clinton Street, Buffalo, NY 14224

© 2024 BookLife Publishing Ltd.

Written by: Doug Barone
Edited by: Elise Carraway
Designed by: Amelia Harris

Cataloging-in-Publication Data

Names: Barone, Doug.
Title: Brazil / Doug Barone.
Description: Buffalo, NY : PowerKids Press, 2025. | Series: Countries of the world | Includes glossary and index.
Identifiers: ISBN 9781499449167 (pbk.) | ISBN 9781499449174 (library bound) | ISBN 9781499449181 (ebook)
Subjects: LCSH: Brazil--Juvenile literature. | Brazil--History--Juvenile literature. | Brazil--Geography--Juvenile literature.
Classification: LCC F2508.5 B376 2025 | DDC 981--dc23

Manufactured in the United States of America

CPSIA Compliance Information: Batch #CW25PK. For further information contact Rosen Publishing at 1-800-237-9932.

Find us on

CONTENTS

Words that look like <u>this</u> can be found in the glossary on page 24.

WHERE IS BRAZIL?

Brazil is located in South America. It is the largest country in South America. The capital city of Brazil is called Brasília.

Brazil

Lots of people live in Brazil. Most of them speak Portuguese, even though many of the countries around them are Spanish-speaking.

LANDSCAPE AND WEATHER

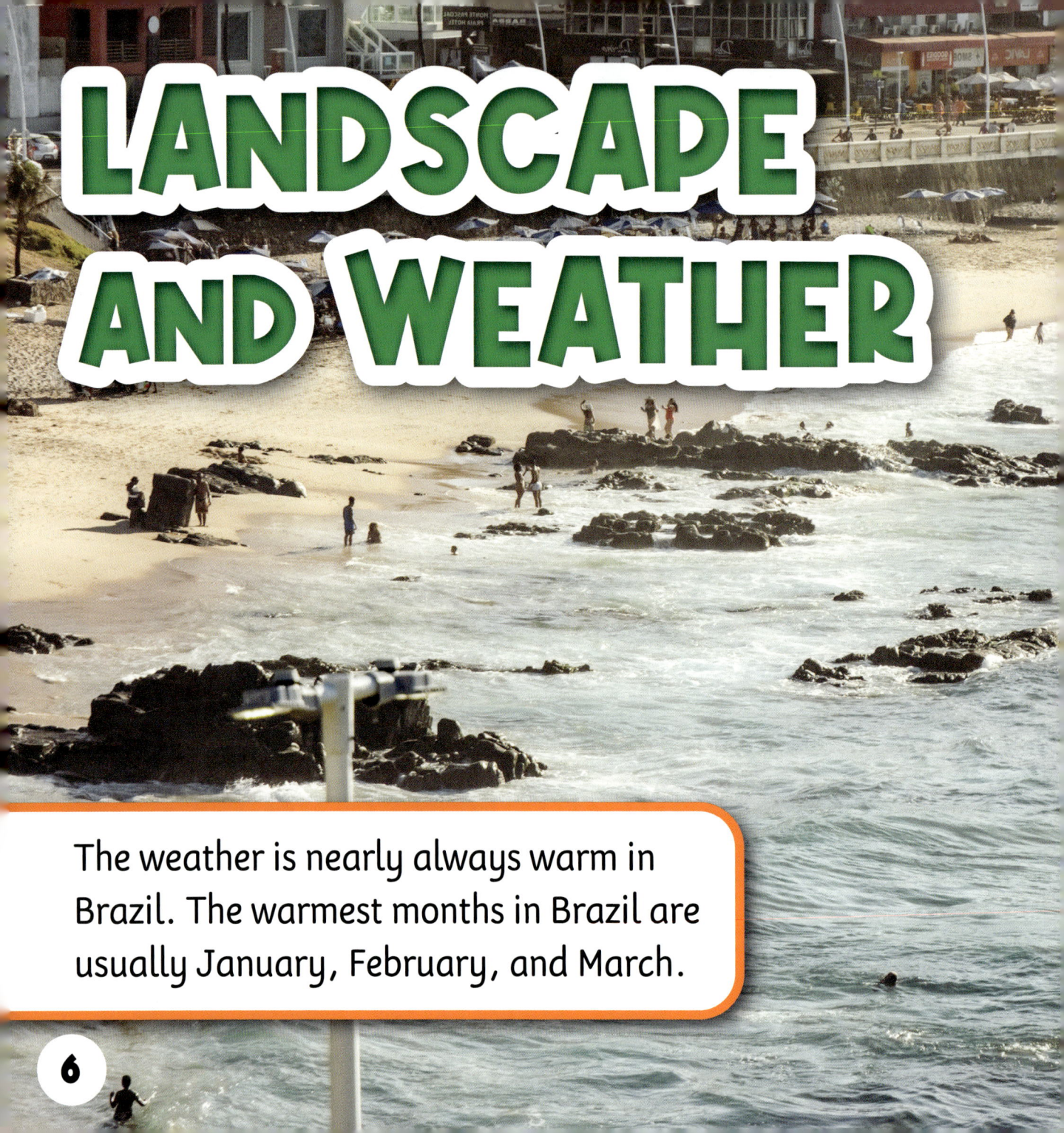

The weather is nearly always warm in Brazil. The warmest months in Brazil are usually January, February, and March.

Over half of Brazil is covered by tropical rainforests, which are very wet. Other parts of Brazil are very dry and are like deserts.

Tropical rainforest

Dry area

RELIGION

The <u>religion</u> with the most followers in Brazil is Christianity. Many of the Christians in Brazil <u>worship</u> in buildings called churches.

Church

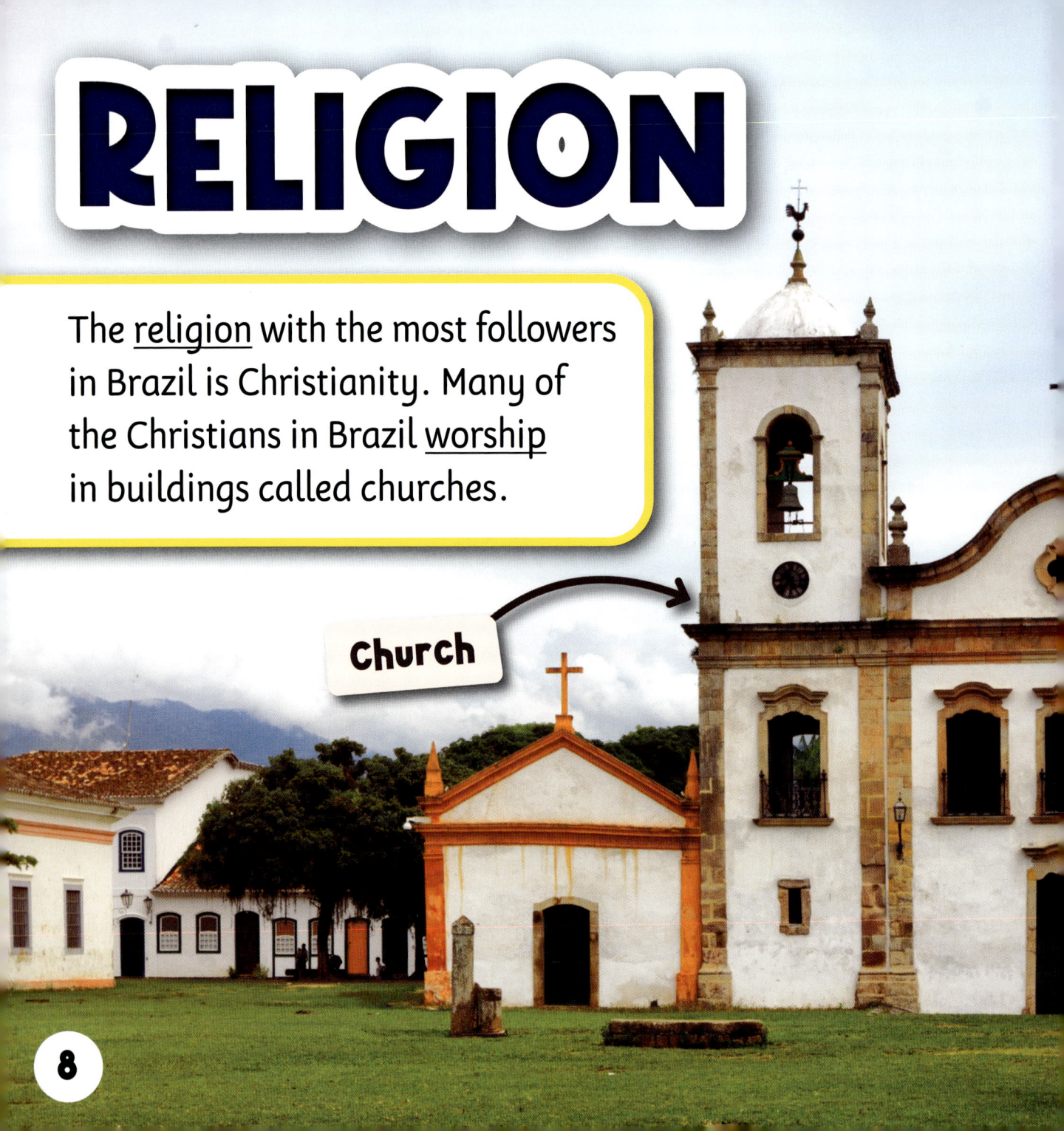

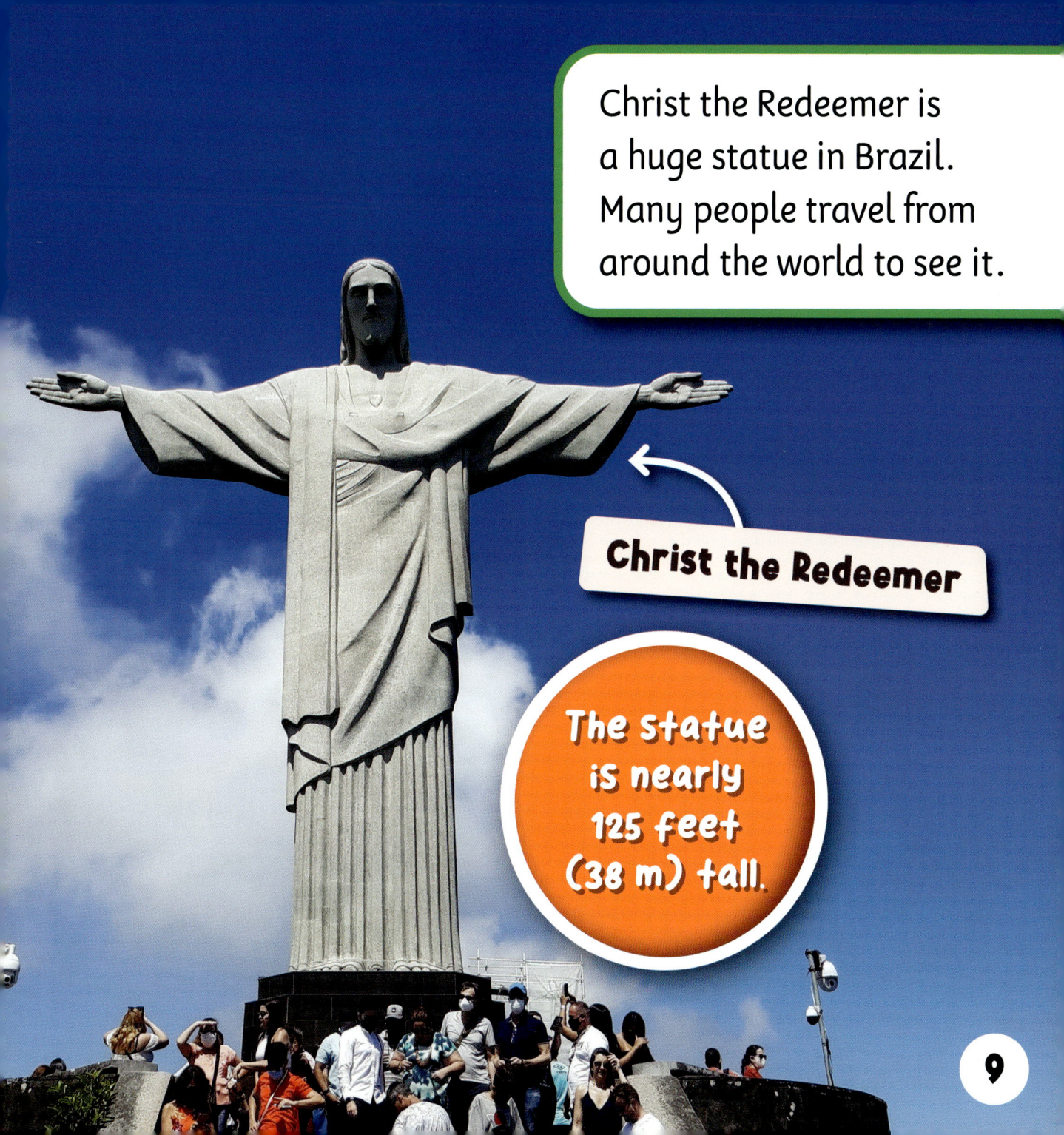

Christ the Redeemer is a huge statue in Brazil. Many people travel from around the world to see it.

Christ the Redeemer

The statue is nearly 125 feet (38 m) tall.

FAMILIES

Most children in Brazil live with their parents and <u>siblings</u>. People often try to live close to their grandparents, aunts, and uncles. In some families, grandparents live in the same house as their children and grandchildren.

In many Brazilian families, both parents go to work. In some families, one parent stays at home to look after the house and the children.

SCHOOL

Children in Brazil must go to school between the ages of 7 and 14. Many start early or stay in school for a few more years. Children often start school at 7 o'clock in the morning.

There are after school clubs in Brazil where children can play sports and music.

13

HOME

Many Brazilians who live in towns or cities live in apartments. At home, children often like to play games and watch television in their free time.

Apartments

Some parts of Brazil are <u>surrounded</u> by rainforest and are very hard to get to. Some of the people who live far away from the cities may not leave the rainforest very often.

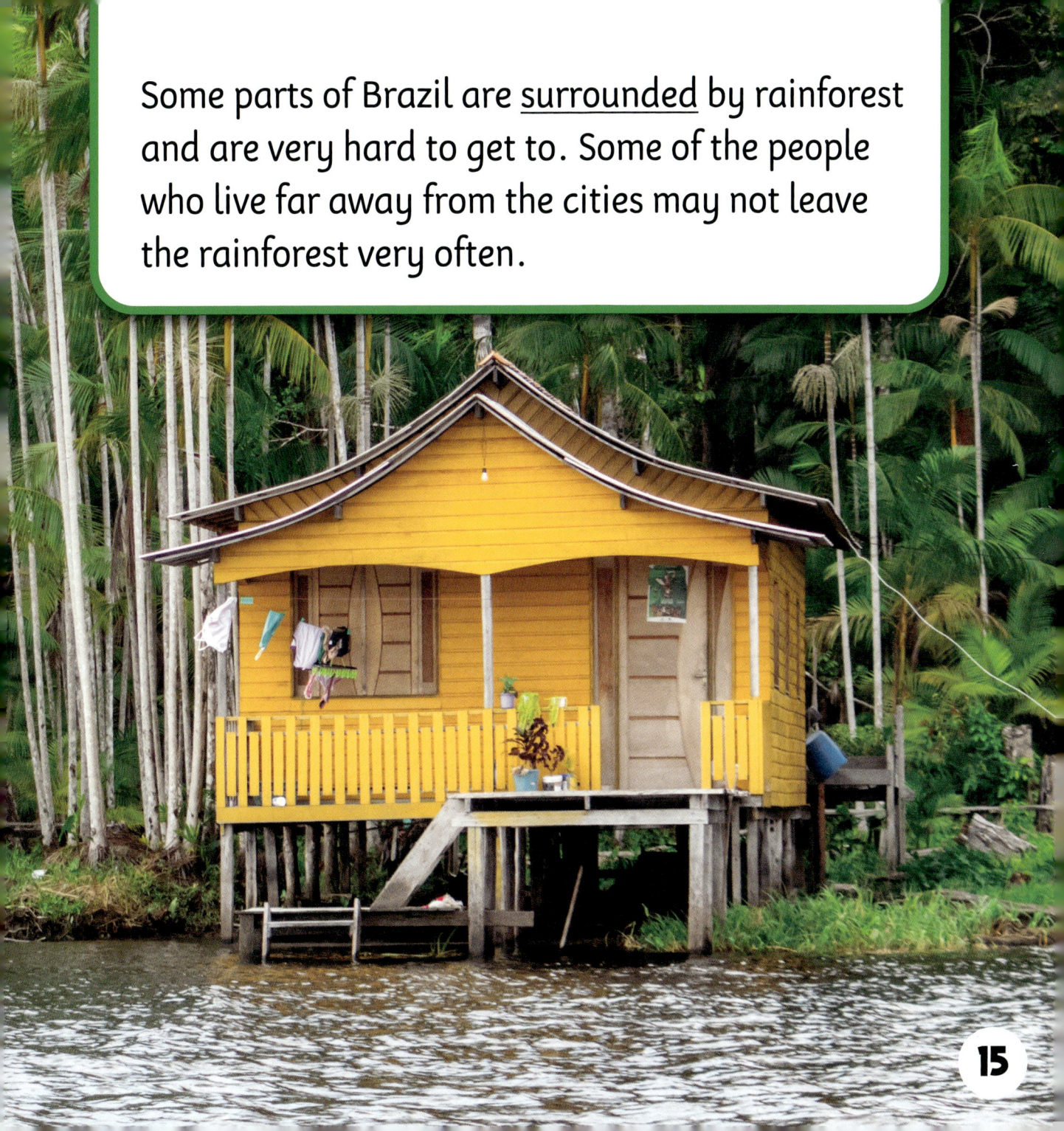

CLOTHING

The <u>traditional</u> style of clothing in Brazil is different from place to place. Many styles of clothing in Brazil are comfortable and colorful.

Headscarf

In some parts of Brazil, many people wear traditional headscarves. People also wear <u>modern</u>, comfortable clothing that suits the warm weather.

SPORTS

Soccer is the most popular sport in Brazil. Brazil's soccer team has won the World Cup many times.

Other popular sports in Brazil include volleyball, basketball, and motorsports.

FOOD

Feijoada is a popular dish in Brazil. It is a stew made from pork and black beans.

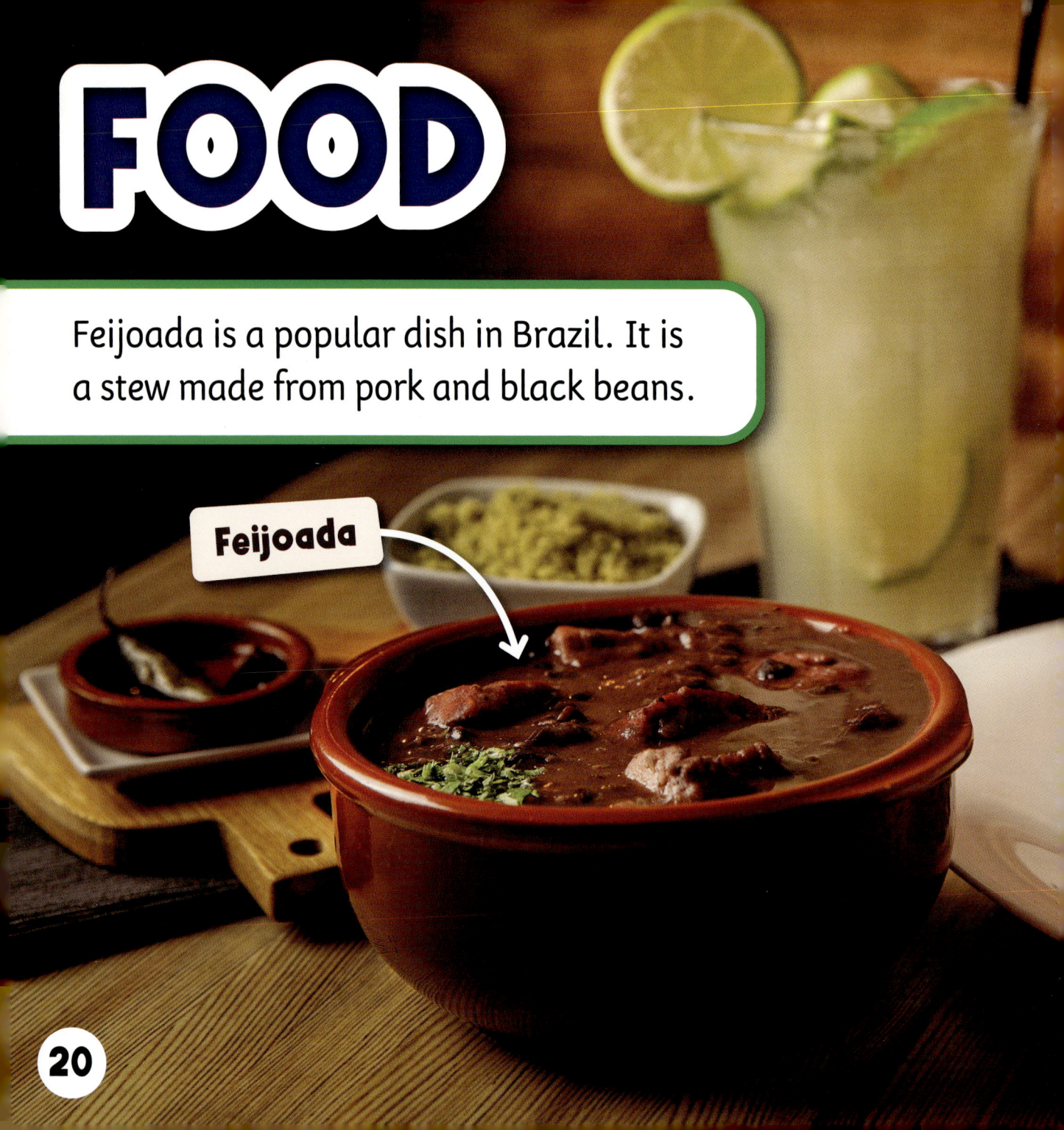

Feijoada

Brazil is also known for its barbecue food. People often barbecue meat and vegetables at home. A special piece of beef called picanha is very popular in Brazil.

FUN FACTS

Brazil is home to many amazing animals, including armadillos, pumas, and tapirs.

Puma

Armadillo

Tapir

There are over 4,000 airports in Brazil.

The Amazon River is in Brazil. It is one of the longest rivers in the world.

GLOSSARY

modern	to do with recent or present times
religion	a system of faith and worship, especially to do with a god or gods
siblings	brothers and sisters
surrounded	covered on every side
traditional	to do with beliefs, customs, or ways of behaving that have been around for a long time
worship	to perform religious acts of praise, such as prayer

INDEX